Cooking Fun

Lae Lae Learns to Cook

Written and Illustrated by Laurenn Prater Barker

The Lae Lae™ Book Series

The Lae Lae™ book series is created by Laurenn Prater Barker
Written and Illustrated by Ms. Barker,
it is a family collaboration in consultation with
advisors in child education, child health and child development.
We hope that the collection is something from which children
will enjoy and learn simple but positive lessons.

The collection is published by Expressions Studio
7040 Avenida Encinas, Ste. 104, Carlsbad, CA 92011

htp://www.laelae.com

ISBN: 978-0-9824172-3-2

Distributed by Expressions Studio

Read Along Story

We meet some new friends in this book. Lae Lae's brother Brent and her mommy are here and her school friends Amalia and Raj are introduced. Raj has moved with his family from India and Amalia has moved from Colombia. Lae Lae's special friend Poco (whom only she can see) and her puppy Patches join in to help Lae Lae learn to cook.

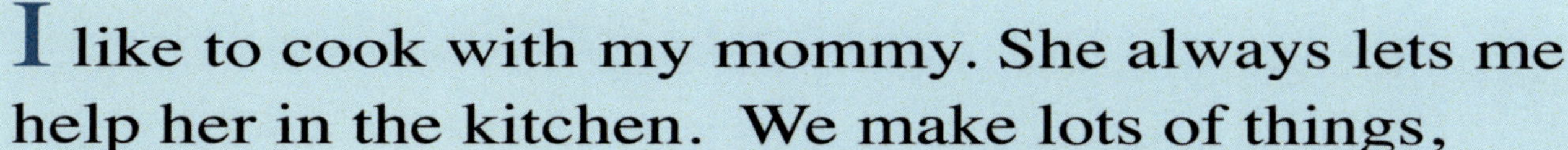

I like to cook with my mommy. She always lets me help her in the kitchen. We make lots of things, like scrambled eggs with broccoli and cheese, teddy bear pancakes, and berry banana smoothies. Sometimes she even lets me think up my own special recipes.

Sometimes when Mommy has extra time or it's a rainy day and I can't go outside, she helps me make something special. We keep a "Lae Lae's Cooking Box" full of goodies to make fun things.

I also have a "Lae Lae's Recipe Book" where I keep all of my favorite recipes. I have some recipes that Mommy liked as a little girl and some that Daddy liked as a little boy and some of my very own like my special cupcakes.

My special cupcakes have nuts and raisins and chocolate chips in them, so we must get flour, sugar and all those things from the grocery store.

When we cook, Mommy reminds me that I have to be careful and everything needs to be clean. I have to wash my hands and wear an apron. I get my special stool to reach the kitchen sink and I "wash up" as Mommy says I should.

Mommy and I have so much fun making my cupcakes. Mommy lets me do so much. I get to put all the stuff in and I get to stir it all up. I like cooking with Mommy.

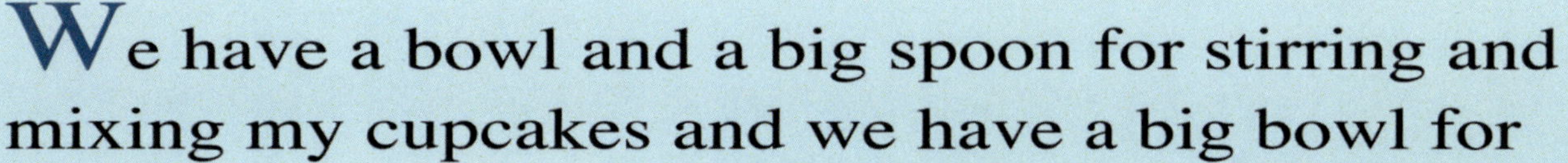

We have a bowl and a big spoon for stirring and mixing my cupcakes and we have a big bowl for mixing the icing too. I try to be very neat but when I get a little extra icing on my hand, it's fun to lick it off.

Patches likes to watch me as I make my cupcakes. I think that she is hoping that I will drop one and she can eat it.

When the cupcakes cool, Mommy shows me how to put the icing on them. I make them white so the sparkles will show up. My friend Poco watches me decorate the cupcakes.

At my school, we have snacks in the afternoon after lunch. We will have a party! I know that my friends Raj and Amalia will really love my cupcakes.

Story Telling Time

Story Telling Time

The following section is designed to encourage your child to develop narrative creativity.

Story telling and a healthy imagination are very important in childhood. After reading about Lae Lae and her cooking experiences your child can be encouraged to invent his or her own stories about cooking or favorite foods.

You can use the Lae Lae story to help your child develop listening and comprehension skills. Children who are introduced to books and stories and then are encouraged to invent and tell their own stories read more easily and at a greater level of comprehension as they progress through school than children who are not.

Use the following pages to encourage your child to add to the story that he or she just read or to create new stories. Encourage freedom and imagination in the interpretation.

For coloring pages from this book and stickers to print on the computer, please visit the website at http://laelae.com.

Lae Lae shows her cupcakes to Patches. But Lae Lae knows that cookies aren't good for her. What do you think she should share with her? Can you tell a story about Lae Lae and Patches?

Poco helps Lae Lae with her pancakes. What do you think Poco wants to add to the pancakes? How would you make your pancakes special?

Lae Lae likes to help her mommy cook. Do you like to cook? What do you cook? Can you make up a recipe to cook?

Lae Lae's big brother Brent likes to cook too. Can you think of a different ending to the story that includes Brent in it?

Cooking Fun

Recipes and Cooking Tips

Notes:

Children are like "living sponges." They soak up all that life gives them. It is our responsibility to give them the best that we can to help them grow into responsible adults. Many childhood experiences are good teachable moments for both the child and the adult. We learn from our children as much as they learn from us.

Cooking Fun provides "Teachable Moments" for Lae Lae and also for your child. Everyone loves freshly cooked treats and gathering around something special that just came from the oven. Cooking is a wonderful way to make a child feel important and appreciated by family members and friends.

Some suggestions for how to enjoy this special time:

1. Let your child help you plan a menu for dinner. Children can learn about healthful foods through meal planning and preparation.

2. Let them tell you about their favorite foods and why they like them. Childhood tastes very greatly; some children like vegetables; some do not. Some children have a sweet tooth; some do not. We can encourage them to favor the better foods by cooking with them creatively.

3. Make a trip to the grocery store or family market to buy what is needed for the meal. You can show your child the different vegetables, fruits, and other products at the store and discuss what each does for the body. Encourage your child to pick out some of the grocery items and tell you why he or she picked them. Is it the size, the bright color, the package design or something else?

4. Lae Lae has a cooking box. It might be fun for your child to develop one. He (boys like to cook too) or she can ask for recipes from family members (like Grandmother's favorite cake from her childhood). Your child can save each recipe and he or she, with your help, can try them out on the family or friends. The box can include photos of foods and recipes that appeal to your child. This can open conversations about how to eat "healthy" and how to choose and eat good food.

5. Cooking is a good time to learn about cleanliness. Ask your child why it is important to wash hands and have a clean cooking area. What are germs? Why are they bad for us? What can we do to help ourselves stay healthy?

6. Let your child help you pick out the bowls and cooking utensils to feel involved with the process. Explain what each one is used for and, if dangerous, how it is dangerous. It is important your child understands how to use the utensils correctly and safely.

7. Cooking is a good time to teach your children about safety. Teach them how pans get hot when on the stove and how they can get burned. Teach them that knives are sharp and can cut.

8. This is a good time to talk to your children about how things can change when cooked or chilled. What happens to vegetables when they are cooked? What happens to juice when it is put in the freezer? It might be fun for your child to make popsicles with juice. What happens when you put liquid cookie dough in the oven? If you have an oven with a see through door, it is fun to watch things cook, rise, spread and change shape.

9. Your children can learn to count by measuring ingredients or counting eggs needed for the recipe. Make a game of it and let them count and put ingredients in the bowl.

10. This is a good time to have a "play" kitchen so your children can practice what they have learned cooking with you. They will mirror you, the teacher. Stop and listen and be amused at their pretend world based on your real world.

11. Use a special occasion to let your children "shine" in the kitchen. Perhaps a Mother's Day or Father's Day would do it. They can plan a special surprise and help you make it and serve it too!

12.The biggest thrill of all will be when children serve up something that they had a hand in making and family or friends compliment them for what they have done. Make it a very special time so they can really feel important.

Match the Item With its Description

PITCHER - this would be used for pouring milk into a bowl. What color is it? Where is the pitcher?

BOWL - This would be used for mixing the ingredients in. What color is it? Where is the bowl?

PLATE - This would be what cookies are placed on to serve to your friends. What color is it? Where is it?

SPOON - This would be used to stir all your ingredients together. What color is it? Where is it?

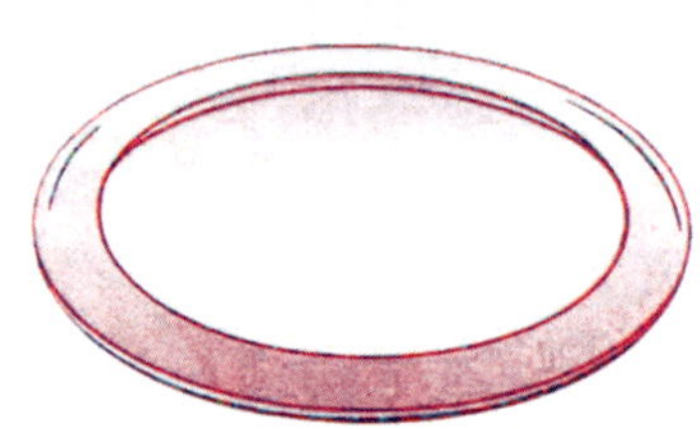

FRYING PAN - This could be used for making teddy bear pancakes. What color is it? Where is it?

Match the Fruit With its Definition and Color

APPLE - Apples are so good for you, fresh, or in a juice or cooked. What color is an apple? Point to the apple.

STRAWBERRY - Strawberries make a smoothie with bananas and blueberries. What color is a strawberry? Point to the strawberries.

LEMON - Lemonade tastes so good in the summertime. What color is a lemon? Point to the lemons.

ORANGE - Juicy and sweet, oranges are very good for you. What color is an orange? Point to the orange.

GRAPES - Grapes are fun to eat one at a time. What color is a grape? Point to the grapes.

How many oranges can you count? Which one is different?
How many apples can you count? Which one is different?

Cooking Tips:

Before starting to cook, it is important to remember some important rules of cooking safety and cleanliness in the kitchen.

Read these tips with a big person before beginning your cooking:

1. Read your recipe carefully to make sure you understand it.
2. Make sure you have all the things your recipe calls for or go to the store to buy them.
3. Make sure the cooking area is clean.
4. Put all the bowls, spoons and things that you will need in the cooking area.
5. Wash your hands and put on a clean apron to cook in.
6. Let a big person help you with the hard stuff - like cutting and handling sharp things. Don't worry, you get to do all the important things - like stirring, and pouring and decorating!
7. Don't overfill the pans and bowls. Things can overflow and make a big mess.
8. Remember that stoves and ovens and the things that are put in them get very hot. Let a big person help you with the hot stuff.
9. Remember that cleaning up afterwards is an important part of your cooking fun; be sure to do it.
10. Put all your cooking things away safely and neatly for the next time.
11. Share with others what you made so they can enjoy it too.

Pear Salad
with Cheese and Honey

INGREDIENTS:

Three firm, ripe pears
1/8 cup honey
Several slices of yellow cheese
Dark green lettuce leaves to cover the plate
Paprika spice

DIRECTIONS:

1. Cut the pears into bite sized cubes.
2. Spread a plate with several large lettuce leaves (the dark ones are better for you).
3. Spread the pear cubes on the lettuce.
4. Drizzle honey all over the pears.
5. Slice and spread slices of cheese.
6. Sprinkle paprika over the cheese.
7. Serve to the family.

Lae Lae's Special Cupcakes

INGREDIENTS:

White cake mix
Eggs (the mix will tell you how many)
White icing mix
1 cup of raisins
Milk (the mix will you how much)
1/2 cup chocolate chips
1 cup of pecan pieces
Cake decorations

DIRECTIONS:

1. Stir the mix with the eggs and milk.
2. Mix in the nuts, chocolate chips and raisins.
3. Put cupcake liners in a cupcake pan.
4. Pour the mix into the liners in the cupcake pan.
5. Have a big person put the cupcakes in the oven.
6. After the cupcakes are cooked, let them cool.
7. Take the cupcakes out and ice them.
8. Decorate the cupcakes with your decorations.
9. Be sure and share them - everybody likes cupcakes.

Teddy Bear Pancakes

INGREDIENTS:

Pancake mix
Eggs for the pancake mix (the mix will tell you how many)
Firm, ripe strawberries (organic is best)
Decorations to make Teddy's eyes, nose and mouth

DIRECTIONS:

1. Put strawberries in a chopping jar and cut them into small pieces.
2. Put the strawberry bits into the pancakes.
3. With a big person's help, pour a big pancake in the middle of the pan (this will be Teddy's head).
4. Pour two little pancakes in the pan (these will be Teddy's ears).
5. When the batter bubbles let a big person turn the pancakes over.
6. When the pancakes are brown, a big person can take them out.
7. Now it's your turn to decorate Teddy as you think he should be.

Scrambled Eggs

with Cheese and Broccoli

INGREDIENTS:

4 Eggs
1/8 cup millk
One cup chopped broccoli (you don't have to have it but it does make the scrambled eggs really good for you!)
Salt and pepper to taste
1/2 cup of shredded cheese
Non stick cooking spray

DIRECTIONS;

1. Break eggs into big bowl.
2. Add milk and stir.
3. Chop broccoli into egg mixture and stir.
4. Spray a frying pan with non-stick cooking spray.
5. Pour mixture into pan and sprinkle top with cheese.
6. Cook over *very* low heat until mixture is firm.
7. Serve for any meal you like.

Berry Banana Smoothie

INGREDIENTS:

1 mashed up banana
1/2 cup of blueberries (organic is best)
1/2 cup of strawberries or blackberries (organic is best)
1 8 oz. container of frozen yogurt
1/2 cup of milk (soy, rice or hemp milk can substitute)
One cherry or extra berry for decoration

DIRECTIONS:

1. Put all ingredients in a blender.
2. Blend everything smooth.
3. Put it in the refrigerator to chill.
4. Serve - yumm good.

Holiday Caterpillar Cookies

INGREDIENTS:

Your favorite cookies (home made ones are yummy)
White icing in a can (you can buy it from the store)
Green and red food coloring
Candy decorations
Walnut chips (these aren't necessary but they are good)

DIRECTIONS:

1. Place cookies in a caterpillar line.
2. Divide white icing into two cups and color one red and one green with food coloring.
3. Spread red and green icing on cookies
4. Decorate with colored sprinkles and nut pieces
5. Add a brown piece of cookie for a nose.
6. Serve to family or friends.

Bright Veggie Salad

INGREDIENTS:

Two big carrots
Two big, firm tomatoes
One big onion
One head of lettuce
Olive oil and lemon to taste
1/2 cup mayonaise
1/4 cup of cranberries
1/4 cup of pine nuts

DIRECTIONS:

1. Chop onions and carrots in a blender on very low speed.
2. Mix onions and carrots in a bowl with mayonaise, olive oil and lemon.
3. Add pine nuts and cranberries.
4. Cut tomatoes in small pieces (let a big person help) and mix in.
5. Chop or shred lettuce and mix with other ingredients.
6. Chill in the refrigerator and then serve.

Let's Read a Food Label

Packaged foods must now be labeled so we can understand what we are buying and make healthy decisions about the foods that we choose.

Look for the label on each box at the grocery store and use it to understand what's inside. Knowing what the nutritional value of the product is helps us buy foods that are healthy for us.

What does this label tell us about the product inside the box? It doesn't have any sugar in it and it has lots of fiber. It doesn't have any trans fat and it has some protein. Ask a big person to explain the label and what it means for you.

Use the information to grow up healthy with good foods to eat.

Nutrition Facts

Serving Size 1/4 cup dry (48g)
(About 1 cup cooked)
Servings Per Container About 8

Amount Per Serving

Calories 170 Calories from Fat 15

	% Daily Value*
Total Fat 1.5g	**2%**
Saturated Fat 0g	**0%**
Trans Fat 0g	
Cholesterol 0mg	**0%**
Sodium 0mg	**0%**
Potassium 100mg	**3%**
Total Carbohydrate 36g	**12%**
Dietary Fiber 2g	**8%**
Sugars 0g	
Protein 4g	

Vitamin A 0% • Vitamin C 0%
Calcium 0% • Iron 2%
Thiamin 10% • Niacin 10%
Folate 4%

*Percent Daily Values are based on a 2,000 calorie diet. Your daily values may be higher or lower depending on your calorie needs:

	Calories:	2,000	2,500
Total Fat	Less than	65g	80g
Saturated Fat	Less than	20g	25g
Cholesterol	Less than	300mg	300mg
Sodium	Less than	2,400mg	2,400mg
Potassium		3,500mg	3,500mg
Total Carbohydrate		300g	375g
Dietary Fiber		25g	30g

Calories per gram:
Fat 9 • Carbohydrate 4 • Protein 4

Cooking Measurements

(good information when you are cooking)

- pinch/dash = less than 1/8 teaspoon
- 3 teaspoons = 1 tablespoon
- 1/4 cup = 4 tablespoons
- 1/3 cup = 5 tablespoons + 1 teaspoon
- 1/2 cup = 8 tablespoons
- 1/2 pint = 1 cup
- 1 cup of dry ingredients = 16 tablespoons
- 1 cup liquid = 8 ounces
- 2 cups liquid = 1 pint
- 4 cups liquid = 1 quart
- 4 quarts liquid = 1 gallon
- 8 ounces = 1 pint
- 16 ounces = 1 pound
- 32 ounces = 1 quart
- 64 ounces = 1/2 gallon

Cooking in Other Countries

Lae Lae has two friends who have moved to her town from other countries. Each country has its own special traditions and foods.

Her friend Amalia has moved with her family from Colombia and Raj has moved with his family from India.

One way to understand and honor other cultures is to try their foods. Lae Lae wants to highlight some recipes that she really likes from Colombia and India. These are very easy for you to make. Many others are on the Internet.

Try them all!

Enjoy!

Arepas
Colombian Corn "Pancakes"

INGREDIENTS:

1 cup water
1 cup cornmeal
1/4 cup parmesan cheese
1/2 cup queso blanco (or farmer's cheese) shredded
1/2 cup colby/monterrey jack cheese shredded
1/4 cup buttermilk

DIRECTIONS:

1. Combine cornmeal and water in a bowl.
2. Add monterrey jack/colby cheese and buttermilk.
3. Heat a non-stick skillet on a very low heat.
4. Drop balls of corn/cheese mixture into pan and flatten into "pancakes" with a spatula.
5. Heat slowly until they are nicely brown.
6. Ask a big person to flip them once to cook them on both sides.
7. Place corn pancakes on a plate and sprinkle queso blanco to melt on top.

Sweet Strawberry Lassi
from India

INGREDIENTS:

1 cup of plain yogurt
1 cup of cold water
1/2 cup strawberries
A pinch of cardamom powder
1 tsp of rose water
A pinch of vanilla flavoring if desired
Sugar to taste
Slivered almonds, pistacios or chocolate chips

DIRECTIONS:

1. Put strawberries, yogurt and very cold water in blender.
2. Add your special flavorings.
3. Mix on high speed until it is frothy.
4. Chill well and serve with slivered almond, pistacio or chip topping.

Oats Payasam
(Indian Oats Porridge)

INGREDIENTS:

Quick oats - 1 cup
cinnamon and nutmeg to taste
Sugar - 1/4 cup
Apple - 1 (chopped into small pieces)
Dates - 1/4 cup chopped
Water - 1 cup

DIRECTIONS:

1. Bring water to a boil with apple and date pieces in it.
2. Add cinnamon, nutmeg, sugar and oats and simmer for five minutes.
3. Add milk and stir again until it is smooth.
4. Serve the porridge warm.

Limonada de Fresa
(Colombian Strawberry Limeade)

INGREDIENTS:

4 cups water
1 cup sugar
1 cup fresh lime juice
ice

DIRECTIONS:

1. Place the strawberries, 2 cups water and sugar in a pot. Cook over medium heat for five minutes. Let the mixture cool and set aside.
2. Place the mixture in a blender with the lime juice, remaining water and ice cubes. Blend and strain into a pitcher.
3. Add ice cubes and pour.

With each book Ms. Barker seeks the advice and consultation of professionals in fields related to child welfare, education and health:

She would like to especially thank the following individuals for their encouragement, support and assistance with the collection.

Dr. Rodrigo A. Munoz, MD - Chair, Advisory Committee
Professor of Psychiatry, University of California, San Diego
Past President, American Psychiatric Association
Private clinical psychiatric practice, San Diego, CA

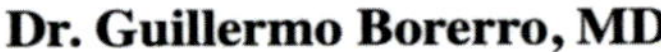

Dr. Guillermo Borerro, MD
Chairman, Department of Psychiatry, Jefferson Regional Medical Center, Clairton, PA
CEO, Guillermo Borrero, MD and Associates, Clairton, PA

Ms. Clara Constain
Pre School and Language Education Specialist
Teacher at public and private secondary schools and university level, Miami, Florida

Ms. Erin Andreasen Kole
M.Ed, Cross Cultural Teaching
San Diego Education Association Board of Directors
English teacher, Marshall Middle School, San Diego, CA

Dr. Kelly O'Bryan, Phd
Licensed Clinical Psychologist, San Diego, California

Dr. Shree Vinekar, MD, LFAACAP
Professor, Department of Psychiatry Associate Chief, Child-Adolescent Mental Health Services
University of Oklahoma College of Medicine, Oklahoma City, Oklahoma

Mr. Paul Weirether
CPS Supervisor II, retired
Child and family counselor and therapist, Central and North Texas

AUTHOR AND ILLUSTRATOR

Laurenn Prater Barker is a lifetime artist and writer having spent more than 30 years in the fields of graphic design and publishing. Her career has incorporated design, illustration, photography and writing. She has designed and produced six books, in addition to the Lae Lae series and more than 100 publications.

Laurenn is also a mother and grandmother and she has been involved extensively in the areas of children's development, both with her own family and on a volunteer basis with public and private organizations.

She is also an accomplished sculptor whose pieces have been featured in numerous national publications and are housed in public and private collections throughout the United States and abroad. Motherhood and the world of children have always been areas of paramount importance to Laurenn. Many of her commissioned works and three of her sculpture collections are dedicated to these subjects (www.expressionsstudio.net).

Laurenn has served on the boards of several organizations dedicated to child and family welfare and she has been involved in children's issues in three states. She has taught art to children and adults, has training in Expressive Arts Therapy and is a member of the International Expressive Arts Therapy Association.

A portion of the proceeds from the Lae Lae collection is donated to organizations that benefit children and animal and environmental causes.

For additional information about Lae Lae and Poco, please visit the web site at http://www.laelae.com

Made in the USA
San Bernardino, CA
30 July 2017